HAIKU MASTER ONITSURA

ONITSURA UEJIMA

TRANSLATED BY
EARL TROTTER

Peach Blossom Press

Peach Blossom Press
Chatham, ON

Cover: Portrait of Onitsura by Yosa Buson (1716–1784)
    In the Kakimori Bunko, Itami City, Hyogo Prefecture.

Uejima Onitsura (1661–1738)
  Haiku Master Onitsura
  Translated by Earl Trotter

  ISBN 978-1-7387466-0-6

1. Uejima Onitsura (1661-1738).   2. Japanese Haiku.

CONTENTS

INTRODUCTION

History of Haiku

Before beginning the discussion, note that the use of "syllable" here is a little different from the usage for English. It could be rendered as "unit of sound". The difference is that, in Japanese, long vowels and double consonants count as 2 syllables and the "n" after a vowel, one. So in romaji "*nan*" is two syllables as is "*shii*" while "*kakko*" is three syllables. Note that the long "e" and long "o" are usually rendered "ei" and "ou" (there are exceptions). The long syllables can also be written with a macron, e.g. "*shī*". As well, "lines" are not lines as in English verse but represent the five or seven (or other) syllabic unit. Japanese verse was traditionally written vertically with no breaks.

The roots of haiku go back to the beginning of Japanese poetry. All the ancient forms consist of five or seven syllables. There were four main types. First there is the *kauta*, in a question and answer format consisting of three lines with the syllabic pattern, 5-7-7. Related is the *sedouka*, basically a double *kauta*. The *chouka* are built of alternating lines of five and seven syllables to an indeterminate length, concluding with a seven-syllable line. Within the *chouka*, there might be a break in the pattern with consecutive five or seven syllable lines. These forms eventually fell out of use although the *chouka* was a prominent form in the Manyoshu (compiled after 759).

Of greater importance are waka (or tanka). It consists of five lines with a syllabic pattern of 5-7-5-7-7. Initially this tended to consist of two couplets and a last line refrain. Later new breakdowns emerged in a 5-7-5 7-7 split where the first three lines modified the last two or where the two parts were related but independent grammatically. Overtime there was also a growing use of a pause after the first line. This gives the first three lines a haiku flavour. By the time of the Kokinshu, compiled in 905, waka was the predominant form. A final point to notice was that the imperial anthologies of waka, over hundreds of years, divided the poems in sections and the four seasons were given prominence.

Beginning in early Heian, there appeared some waka where one person would compose the first three lines and another person, the last two. Such are called renga, or linked verse. This was mainly an exercise in wit. However the practice continued and slowly developed. Verses began to become linked – one writer composing a 5-7-5 opening then another adding 7-7, then 5-7-5 and so on. Eventually one hundred links became the standard. The first five lines would have a certain meaning, but lines four to eight would change the core idea, then lines six to ten likewise. By 1200 renga was a distinct genre. A group of poets would meet and then compose spontaneously to the preceding verse. Renga developed very complex rules for linking and also developed season words, or *kigo,* to be followed. The opening three lines were deemed very important and called *hokku. Hokku* were sometimes published separately and this gave them their own identity.

From renga, a humorous form developed, *haikai no renga,* which we will hereafter refer simply as *haikai.* The opening verse, as in renga, is called *hokku.* In addition to humour and wit, it also employed more colloquial language. Renga had followed the diction of traditional waka poets. The change here can also be traced to a shift where the merchant class became more involved in poetry. In Heian times it was limited to aristocrats. The first school of haikai was the Teimon School founded by Teitoku (1570-1653). Basically their principles were identical to renga, with most of its complex rules intact, with the exception of the use of colloquial language.

A reaction set in against the complexities of the Teimon School and Soin (1604-1682) founded the Danrin School. This school sought freedom and almost any diction and subject matter, including vulgar language and obscenities, were used. There was a heated competition between the two schools. Through all this development was the increasing focus on the independent *hokku.*

Although a later appellation (see below), we will refer to the independent *hokku* as haiku henceforth given it ubiquitousness use.

The course of haiku was changed forever with the appearance of Matsuo Basho (1644–1694). He promoted the use of ordinary language as means of sincere expression. As well, subject matter was broadened from the Teimon School, along with humour, but not to the excesses of the Danrin School. Basho promoted a series of various approaches to *haiku* – in fact, not staying put in one theory was part of his aesthetic. He talked of sincerity (*makoto*) and later lightness (*karumi*) and his poems often exhibited *sabi* and *wabi* – feelings of transience, imperfection, poverty and simplicity. Basho had many disciples, the major being Takarai Kikaku who wrote a moving account of Basho's last days and was influential until the time of Buson.

Basho was based in Edo. In the Kansai region (Kyoto, Osaka), Uejima Onitsura (1661–1738 wrote a poetics of haiku based on sincerity (*makoto*). His and Basho's ideas are likely connected in some manner, if only through Onitsura's contacts with Basho's disciples. Onitsura will be dealt with in some detail below.

The two major haiku poets after Basho were Yosa Buson (1716–1784) and Kobayashi Issa (1763–1828). Buson was a poet known for his sensibility and lyricism. He sought to be natural, not encumbered by too many rules. In his lifetime he was more renown for his paintings and he is considered a master of *haiga*, a form of painting incorporating haiku aesthetics tending to a simple (though not simplistic) style. Issa, who was not well known in his lifetime is the foremost poet of humanity imbued with an atmosphere of pathos. There is also much down-to-earth humour in many of his haiku. Tan Taigi (1709-1771), a contemporary of Buson is another notable poet. The finest woman haiku poet is considered to be Chiyo-ni (Kaga no Chiyo) (1703-1775).

The bridge to the modern era came with Masaoka Shiki (1867–1902). Considered one of the four great haiku poets, along with Basho, Buson and Issa, Shiki was the one to designate what had been known as *hokku*, as haiku. He favoured haiku based on a realistic observation of nature. Shiki revivified the haiku form. It has not only been exceedingly popular in Japan since his death but enjoys a popularity worldwide.

Characteristics of Haiku

Haiku can be succinctly summarized as a Japanese poetic form consisting of seventeen syllables in a 5-7-5 format, which will include a season word (*kigo*) and a "cutting word" (*kireji*). As mentioned previously, the syllable is a "sound unit" and the 5-7-5 format, rendered in lines, in English, is not done so in Japanese. Haiku usually cover some aspect of nature, even if talking about a social event, not the least, because of the season word. Haiku will usually be in two parts, either the first line versus the last two, or first two lines versus the last. The cutting word often serves to build this structure (end of line one, two, or three) and as well frequently highlights the preceding phrase (like an exclamation mark).

Since Basho and Onitsura, haiku has been seen as representing the true feelings and/or experience of the poet. However, this should not be seen as being solely a spontaneous insight into life or nature, immediately rendered down as haiku (the Zen moment). Haiku, even of masters such as Basho, are constantly revised in composition and certain events are, in fact, imaginary (viz. certain episodes in Basho's *The Narrow Road to the Deep North*). However, the best haiku will certainly be insightful and represent the poet's true feelings, an aesthetic that goes back to the earliest writings of Chinese and Japanese aesthetics (see the Mao Commentary to the *Book of Songs* and the *Preface* to the *Kokinshu*).

Uejima Onitsura (上島鬼貫)

Onitsura was born in 1661 in Itami (now in Hyogo Prefecture). His family, of samurai descent, was involved in the *sake* brewing business. He was interested in haiku from an early age and wrote his first haiku at age seven (Western style age). At twelve, he studied with Matsue Shigeyori (1602–1680), a haiku writer and editor originally from Kyoto, who later moved to the Osaka area.

Shigeyori had affiliations at various times with both the Teimon and Danrin schools. Later, at age sixteen, Onitsura joined the Danrin school and met its master, Soin in 1680.

At twenty-five he withdrew from the haiku circles, seeking a deeper meaning in haiku. This self-searching lasted five years, after which he reached his initial realization of *makoto*. Also at age twenty-five he went to Osaka to study medicine. He then served at various locations as a doctor along with other duties. He met disciples of Basho and through them became familiar with Basho's writing. There are conflicting views on his exact relationship to Basho. Onitsura's eldest son (he had two others) died at age six in 1700. A few of his haiku reflect his son's passing. He wrote his famous treatise on haiku, *Hitorigoto* (Soliloquy), in 1718. Onitsura died, in what is now Osaka, in 1738.

Onitsura is more famous today for his theory of *makoto* (sincerity) than for his haiku. He felt that *makoto* had to be developed by rigorous training and that its expression from the heart rather than through clever words was essential. A poem with *makoto* will transcend time and the changing styles of poetry. Basho also employed *makoto* in his aesthetics and his conception is not incompatible with Onitsura's. The following are some of Onitsura's teachings from *Hitorgoto* (based on the Crowley translation – see Further Reading):

- The Way of *haikai* appears to be shallow, but is deep; it appears to be simple, but is difficult.
- If haikai is to accomplish its role as a means to achieve *makoto*, you must concentrate and practice diligently.
- … treat everyone in the world as your brother or sister. Compare *haikai* to actions in daily life, and think of *haikai* as something in harmony with everyday things. Each verse will then emerge naturally.
- How can there be any *makoto* if there is no feeling of great joy in aspects of nature in your poetry?
- … compose poetry thinking passionately and deeply, and employ whatever naturally comes to mind [paraphrased slightly. Ed.].
- The path of training is endless …

- … concentrate on neither avoiding falsehood nor including *makoto* – the result is that there is no falsehood in any verse and *makoto* emerges naturally. This is because there is no deception in the normal human heart, and people are naturally endowed with profound understanding of the pathos of things (aware 哀れ).
- By practicing *haikai* a person is able to realize *makoto*, and even insensitive people will come to know true feeling.
- … the verses of a poet who has earnestly practiced the Way of *makoto* will not seem outdated, no matter how many years have passed since they were written.
- Good poems are those in which the language and spirit are in harmony.
- There is no haikai without *makoto*.

Onitsura's mature haiku then, sought to achieve the principles of *makoto*. He often uses simple diction and events from everyday life. There is a similarity in his approach and that of the Chinese poets (e.g. Mei Yaochen (1002–1060)) espousing "blandness" as a poetic virtue. His haiku tend to be regular with seventeen syllables and a season word although there are exceptions. There is also a fine touch of humour in many of his haiku.

The Translation

The translation of the haiku is fairly literal. I have tried to follow the original images sequentially but with Japanese this is not always feasible. The important point is to make the key image clearly stand out. The form is reflected in the three-line structure but no attempt has been made for a consistent number of syllables or accents per line. The Japanese text is from various sources on the internet including university archives but a few were transcribed from Blyth. Haiku from different sources matched, other than the use of kanji versus hiragana in some instances. Some 428 haiku are translated from the approximately 800 that have been preserved. The haiku are arranged by, but not within, season.

The romaji is for general guidance only. I have replaced the sound of the older forms, は*(ha)*, へ*(he)*, ひ*(hi)*, and ふ*(fu)*, where applicable, as they are now, in many instances, わ*(wa)*, え*(e)*, い*(i)*, and う*(u)*. The archaic ゐ*(wi)* is *i* in modern Japanese. Note that ふ *(fu)* was often used as a verb ending where う*(u)* is now employed. There are also the following older stand-alone forms that are retained in modern Japanese but have a different sound: は*(ha)*, へ *(he)* and を*(wo)* as *wa* (topic marker), *e* (to) and *o* (object marker) respectively. As well, the pre-modern rendering of "today" as けふ *(kefu)* has been replaced by *kyou* in the romaji.

Further Reading

There is not a lot of material on Onitsura in English. The six Blyth volumes have many haiku by Onitsura scattered throughout their pages. There is a chapter in *A History of Haiku*, Vol. 1 (pp. 97-104) that deals specifically with Onitsura and is highly recommended (as are all of Blyth's works on haiku). Crowley's piece is a translation and commentary on Onitsura's prime prose work *Soliloquy* and is essential reading for understanding *makoto*. A final article on Onitsura is by Qiu, discussing Daoist influences. The Japanese entry is a selection of Onitsura's work including 357 haiku as well as prose pieces.

The other entries for further reading relate to haiku in general and to the four most noted poets, Basho, Buson, Issa and Shiki. Yasuda's volume was of great help in doing the Introduction. As well, Lanoue's website of Issa translations was useful in resolving certain ambiguities in the text where the same term was used by both Onitsura and Issa. Of course, this list is just a fraction of the works available.

Blyth, R. H. *Haiku*. 4 Vols. Tokyo: The Hokuseido Press, 1949–1952.

_____. *A History of Haiku*. 2 Vols. Tokyo: The Hokuseido Press, 1963–1964.

Crowley, Cheryl. "Putting Makoto Into Practice. Onitsura's Hitorigoto" *Monumenta Nipponica*, Vol. 50, No. 1, (Spring 1995), 1-46.

Higginson, William J. *The Haiku Handbook*. New York: McGraw-Hill Book Company, 1985.

Lanoue, David. *Haiku of Kobayashi Issa*. http://haikuguy.com/issa/

Masaoka Shiki. *Selected Poems*. Translated by Burton Watson. New York: Columbia University Press, 1997.

Matsuo Basho. *Basho's Haiku*. 2 Vols. Translated by Toshiharu Oseko. Saitama: Toshiharu Oseko, 1990-1996.

_____. *The Complete Haiku*. Translated by Jane Reichhold. Tokyo: Kodansha International Ltd., 2008.

McElligot, Patrick. (1970). *The Life and Work of Kobayashi Issa*. Doctoral Dissertation at the School of Oriental and African Studies, London. ProQuest Dissertations Publishing.

Qiu, Peipei. "Onitsura's Makoto and the Daoist Concept of the Natural" *Philosophy East and West*, Vol. 51, No. 2, (Apr. 2001), 232-246.

Sawa, Yuki, & Shiffert, Edith. *Haiku Master Buson*. San Francisco: Heian International Publishing Company, 1978.

Yasuda, Kenneth. *The Japanese Haiku*. Boston: Tuttle Publishing, 1957.

上島鬼貫. 鬼貫句選・独ごと. 東京: 岩波書店, 2010.

New Year

ほんのりとほのや元日なりにけり
honnori to ho no ya ganjitsu nari ni keri

> Creeping up,
>> almost unnoticed –
>>> it's New Year's Day!

搗杵に血を見る餅のつよさかな
kachigine ni chi o miru mochi no tsuyosa kana

> Pounding with the mallet
>> I spot some blood
>>> – that *mochi*'s[1] tough!

我宿の春は来にけり具足餅
waga yado no haru wa ki ni keri gusokumochi

> At my house
>> spring[2] has arrived
>>> – *gusoku mochi*[3]!

_____

[1]   Rice cakes, eaten all year but associated especially with New Year's.
[2]   In fact spring means New Year's here.
[3]   Onitsura was of samurai descent and *gusoku mochi* (rice cake) was presented to the suit of armour in one's home and that may be what is reflected here.

六日八日中に七日のなづな[4]かな
muika youka naka ni nanuka no nazuna kana

> Between the sixth day and eighth day,
>   that is, the seventh day,
>   – shepherd's purse[5]!

しだ売りて夜るあたま剃る山家かな
shida urite yoru atama soru yamaga kana

> The seller of ferns,
>   shaves his head in the evening,
>   at his mountain home.

初日影まづ出でたりな生駒山
hatsunichi kage mazu idetari na ikomayama

> Sunrise on New Year's Day.
>   Its shadow was first to appear
>   – Mt. Ikoma[6]!

---

[4]   Modern usage is なずな (薺).
[5]   One of the herbs (the "seven spring jewels") added to a porridge eaten on the 7th day of the 1st lunar month for its health benefits.
[6]   Near Nara.

高砂や去年を捨てつつ初むかし
takasago ya kozo o sute tsutsu hatsu mukashi

    In Takasago[7] –
        leaving behind last year
            while still thinking of it[8].

五器の香や春立つけふの餅機嫌
goki no kou ya harutatsu kyou no mochi kigen

    Five incense burners going!
        This first day of spring
            I'm in the mood for *mochi*[9].

嘉儀候よやおら初日の梅心
kagi soro yo yaora shonichi no umegokoro

    Season of celebration –
        suddenly, plum buds
            in the New Year's sunrise.

---

[7]   Now a city in Hyogo Prefecture.
[8]   The expression 初むかし is used for thinking about the old year on New Year's Day.
[9]   Rice cakes associated with the New Year.

門松やうしろに笑ふ武庫の山
kadomatsu ya ushiro ni warau muko no yama

    Laughter
        from behind the *kadomatsu*[10] –
            the hills of Muko[11].

とし木めせおくのおく山馬の声
toshi ki mese oku no oku yama uma no koe

    Gazing at the New Year's tree[12],
        from deep in the hills
            the neighing of horses.

火の数や年徳棚の賑やかさ
hi no kazu ya toshitokudana no nigiyaka sa

    Lamps all lit –
        busy setting up
            the shelf for the New Year's God.

---

[10]   Traditional New Year's decorations using pine (now bamboo) and placed outside the entrance in pairs to welcome ancestral spirits and *kami* (gods) of the harvest.

[11]   In Kyoto Prefecture, for a brief time site of the pre-Heian imperial capital.

[12]   *Kadamatsu.*

去年より物一時も忘られぬ
kyonen yori mono itsutoki mo wasurarenu

    I don't forget
       even one thing
          from last year.

中垣や梅にしらける去年の雲
nakagaki ya ume ni shirakeru kozo no kumo

    By the fence,
       the plum blossoms are as white
         as last year's clouds.

卯の花の糸に先づよる初音かな
unohana no ito ni sakizu yoru hatsune kana

    Strings of bean-curd lees
       the night before
         the first warbling of the New Year.

うちはれて障子も白し初日影
uchi harete shouji mo shiroshi hatsuhikage

    At our place, it's cleared up
       and the *shoji*[13] are white –
          sunshine on New Year's morning.

小雨降るとんども例の火影かな
kosame furu tondomo rei no hokage kana

    Light rain falling –
       silhouettes against the fire
          burning the New Year's decorations[14].

土ふるや神の若菜に鈴女
tsuchi furu ya kami no wakana ni suzume

    The earth shakes –
       sparrows
          in the fresh spring greens[15] of the gods.

---

[13]   A sliding door or partition in a Japanese house, usually with white translucent panels.

[14]   The New Year's gate decorations were burned on the 15th day.

[15]   Seven different herbs were picked on the 6th day of New Year's for making rice cakes (*mochi*) and rice gruel, eaten the next day.

春の野に蹲踞てゐるわかなつむ
haru no no ni sonkyote iru wakana tsumu

    In the spring field
       I squat down
          and pick the fresh greens.

笋は穂に出る雲の初音かな
takanna wa ho ni deru kumo no hatsune kana

    The tips of bamboo shoots come out.
       On a cloudy day
          the first warbling of the year.

大旦昔吹きにし松の風
ooashita mukashi fukinishi matsu no kaze

    New Year's Day!
       As in ancient times,
          wind blowing through the pines.

Spring

状見れば江戸も降りけり春の雨
jou mireba edo mo furi keri haru no ame

> I see in the letter
> > it is also falling in Edo[16] –
> > > spring rain.

骸骨の上を粧て花見かな
gaikotsu no ue o yosobi de hanami kana

> Skeletons
> > all dressed up in their finest
> > > for cherry blossom viewing!

庭前に白く咲いたる椿かな
niwa mae ni shiroku saitaru tsubaki kana

> At the front of the garden
> > those white blossoms
> > > – the camellias!

---

[16] Old name for Tokyo.

青麥や雲雀があがるあれ下がる
aomugi ya hibari ga agaru are sagaru

> The green barley!
>   The skylark soars,
>   then descends.

春の水ところどころに見ゆる哉
haru no mizu tokorodokoro ni miyuru kana

> The spring run-off,
>   over here, over there,
>   it can be seen everywhere!

としひとつ又もかさねつ梅の花
toshi hitotsu mata mo kasa netsu ume no hana

> This year once more
>   a parasol for the heat
>   – plum blossoms!

すつと立つ草木の中に松の花
sutsu to tatsu kusaki no naka ni matsu no hana

scattered about and standing
amidst the vegetation
– pine cones.

鶯よいつをむかしの雪の声
uguisu yo itsu o mukashi no yuki no koe

The bush warbler
in times past,
the voice of the snow.

鶯が梅の小枝に糞をして
uguisu ga ume no koeda ni kuso o shite

The bush warbler
pooped
on a small plum branch.

そのそこにおのれを梅に烏とは
sono soko ni onore o ume ni karusu to wa

Right there,
just perching in the plum tree,
there's a crow

鶯や音を入れて只青き鳥
uguisu ya oto o irete tada aoki tori

The bush warbler!
It starts to sing,
just an ordinary greenish bird.

とび鮎の底に雲行く流れかな
tobi ayu no soko ni kumo iku nagare kana

The sweetfish leaps up
while right below it,
clouds go flowing by!

鶯よ花は散るとも飛びまはれ
uguisu yo hana wa chirutomo tobi ma hare

    A bush warbler
        as blossoms fall, flies off
            in the fine weather.

山里や井戸の端なる梅の花
yamazato ya ido no hashita naru ume no hana

    A mountain village –
        by the edge of the well,
            plum blossoms!

鳥はまだ口もほどけず初桜
tori wa mada kuchi mo hodokezu hatsu sakura

    The birds have yet
        to open their beaks
            – the first cherry blossoms!

あふみにもたつや湖水の春霞
afumi ni mo tatsu ya kosui no harugasumi

In Afumi[17]
spring mist again hovers
over the lake.

夕暮は鮎の腹見る川瀬かな
yuugure wa ayu no hara miru kawase kana

In the evening
I see the bellies of sweetfish
in the river shallows.

雨だれや暁がたに帰る雁
amadare ya akatsuki gata ni kaeru kari

Raindrops!
At the break of day,
migrating geese.

17   Ancient name for Omi province, now Shiga Prefecture. The lake in question
      is Lake Biwa.

谷水や石も歌詠む山桜
tanimizu ya ishi mo uta yomu yamazakura

    The stream in the valley –
        rocks too, chant poems
            on the mountain cherry blossoms.

鶯の青き音をなく梢かな
uguisu no aoki oto o naku kozue kana

    The sound of the green bush warbler
        singing
            from the treetops!

麦蒔や妹が湯をまつ頬かぶり
mugimaki ya imouto ga yu o matsu houkaburi

    Barley sowing season!
        Younger sister waits her turn for the hot bath
            with her headscarf still on.

膝合す雛の背中を初めかな
hiza awasu hina no senaka o hajime kana

    The back of the knee joint
       of a baby chick -
           where does it begin?

鳶からす蛙が母も水かがみ
tonbi karasu kaeru ga haha mo mizu kagami

    A black kite and crows,
       a mother frog too,
          – all reflected in the pond.

梅が香や衆生にみちて軒の声
umegaka ya shujou ni michite noki no koe

    The scent of plums!
       The sound from the houses
          bustling with life.

物すごやあらおもしろや帰り花
monosugo ya ara omoshiro ya kaeri hana

    Amazing!
        Interesting!
           – the flowers on my way home.

豆喰うてまめの花とも詠ばや
mame kuute mame no hana tomo nagameba ya

    What if I compose a poem
        on the bean blossoms
           while eating beans!

この塚は柳なくてもあはれなり
kono tsuka wa yanagi nakute mo aware nari

    This grave,
        without the willow,
           would still be sorrowful.

老も花と流るゝ年のます鏡
rou mo hana to nagaruru toshi no masu kagami

> Old age and flowers --
>> a mirror of the years
>>> flowing by.

葉なりとも西吟桜ふところに
ha nari tomo saigin sakura futokoro ni

> When the leaves come out
>> the cherry blossoms remain yet
>>> in Saigin's[18] bosom.

梅散つてそれより後は天王寺
ume chitsute sore yori nochi wa tennouji

> After the plum blossoms
>> have fallen –
>>> Tennoji Temple[19].

---

[18]   A haiku poet who died in 1709. He was close to Saikaku and knew Onitsura.
       Cherry blossoms appear before the leaves come out.
[19]   Presumably Shitennoji Temple in Osaka.

日南にも尻のすはらぬ猫の妻
hinata ni mo shiri no suwaranu neko no tsuma

    Even at high noon
        she doesn't sit on her ass
            – cat in heat[20]!

白魚や目までしら魚目は黒魚
shirauo ya me made shirauo me wa kurouo

    The whitefish[21]!
        Except for the eyes it's a white fish –
            but it's eyes are those of a blackfish!

猫の目のまだ昼過ぎぬ春日かな
neko no me no mada hirusuginu kasuga kana

    By the cat's eyes
        it's not yet past noon,
            this spring day.

---

[20] Literally "the cat's wife", a euphemism for a cat in heat.
[21] Almost certainly the icefish.

夢返せ烏の覚ます霧の月
yume kaese karasu no samasu kiri no tsuki

Give back my dream!
Crows have wakened me
to a misty moon.[22]

野田村に蜆あへけり藤の頃
nodamura ni shijimi ahe keri fuji no koro

In Wistaria Village[23],
it's clam season
when wistaria is in bloom.

又もまた花にちられてうつらうつら
mata mo mata hana ni chirarete utsurautsura

Again and again
the blossoms fall –
dozing off.

---

[22] Onitsura's death haiku. It has been variously interpreted.
[23] Actually Noda, now a city in Chiba, whose kanji characters combined with
      "*fuji*", mean Japanese wisteria.

麦藁は麦はく庭の箒きかな
mugiwara wa mugi haku niwa no houki kana

    The garden broom
        that sweeps the wheat
            is made of wheat straw.

樹の中にただ青柳の尾長鳥
ki no naka ni tada aoyagi no onagatori

    Right in the middle of the grove
        there's a rooster
            on a budding willow.

麦の穂も赤らむ物を法の声
mugi no ho mo akaramu mono o norinokoe

    Even ears of wheat
        turn red
            at the preaching of the priest.

面影はしらぬ翁の花香かな
omokage wa shiranu okina no hanaka kana

    People's faces,
        pretending not to notice
            the gentleman's flowery scent.

目は横に鼻は竪なり春の花
me wa yoko ni hana wa tate nari haru no hana

    Eyes are horizontal
        noses are vertical –
            spring blossoms!

あちらむけ後もゆかし花の色
achira muke ushiro mo yukashi hana no iro

    Even turning my back to them,
        still enchanting
            is the colour of the flowers.

木も草も世界みな花月の花
ki mo kusa mo sekai mina kagetsu no hana

> The trees have them and plants too –
>> everywhere
>>> – blossoms of February[24]!

北へ出れば東へでれば花だらけ
kita e dereba higashi e dereba hana darake

> If you go north,
>> if you go east,
>>> – flowers everywhere.

梅の花の目にもたまらで網引か
ume no hana no me ni mo tamara de abiki ka

> Are they eyeing the plum blossoms
>> as they haul in
>>> the fishing nets?

---

[24] The second lunar month, literally "Flower Month".

杖ついた人は立ちけり梨子の花
tsue tsuita hito wa tachikeri nashi no hana

   A woman, clutching her cane,
     stands up –
       pear blossoms!

曙や麦の葉末の春の霜
akebono ya mugi no hazue no haru no shimo

   Dawn!
     Spring frost
       on the tips of the barley.

かけまはる夢や焼野の風の音
kakemawaru yume ya yake no no kaze no oto

   Meandering dreams –
     the sound of the wind
       over the burnt fields.

松や竹みどりの中に木瓜つつじ
matsu ya take midori no naka ni boke tsutsuji

    Amidst the green
      of the pine and bamboo –
         flowering quince and azalea.

水入れて鉢にうけたる椿かな
mizu irete hachi ni uketaru tsubaki kana

    Getting the vase
      and filling it with water –
         the camellia!

窓ひらけ幸ありのみのかへり花
mado hirake kou ari no mi no kaeri hana

    Opening the window,
      fortune smiles on me –
         blossoms have returned!

かた顔や見ぬおく山の花の色
kata kao ya minu okuyama no hana no iro

    Looking that way
        one can't see the colour of the flowers
            of Okuyama[25].

順ふや音なき花も耳の奥
matsurau ya otonaki hana mo mimi no oku

    I obey!
        The soundless flowers too
            pervade my ears.

桜咲くころ鳥足二本馬四本
sakura saku koro tori ashi nihon uma yonhon

    When cherry blossoms bloom –
        birds have two legs,
            horses have four!

---

[25]   In Nara Prefecture.

咲くからに見るからに花のちるからに
saku karani miru karani hana no chiru karani

    The cherry blossoms flower
        so I gaze upon them
            so they fall – so…

口なしに鼻うちかみて窓の花
kuchi nashi ni hana uchi kamite mado no hana

    Mouth covered,
        blowing my nose –
            blossoms by the window!

春ならば朧月とも詠めうに
haru naraba oborozuki tomo nagameu ni

    If a hazy moon appears
        this spring,
            together, let's compose haiku.

桜さくと遠山見こせ眉の八
sakura saku to touyama mi kose mayu no hachi

    Cherry blossoms in bloom.
        Looking across to the distant mountains
           – figure eight eyebrows[26].

春立や星の中から松の色
haru tatsu ya hoshi no naka kara matsu no iro

    The beginning of spring!
        From the midst of the stars,
           the hue of pines.

春風や三保の松原清見寺
haru kaze ya miho no matsubara kiyomidera

    Spring breeze!
        Miho no Matsubara[27]!
           Kiyomidera[28]!

---

[26]   Eyebrows shaped like 八.
[27]   A famous beach and pine grove in Shizuoka Prefecture.
[28]   A noted Buddhist temple in Kyoto.

うつろふや日向の花に陰の花
utsurou ya hinata no hana ni kage no hana

Fading!
　Flowers in the sunlight,
　　flowers in the shade.

春の夜の枕嗅ぐやら目が腫れた
haru no yo no makura kagu yara me ga hareta

Spring night –
　in bed sniffling,
　　eyes all swollen.

近江にも立つや湖水の春霞
oumi ni mo tatsu ya kosui no haru gasumi

In Omi Province[29],
　spring mist, once again,
　　forms over the lake.

---

[29]　Now Shiga Prefecture. The lake is Lake Biwa.

山吹はさかで蛙は水の底
yamabuki wa saka de kaeru wa mizu no soko

> *Yamabuki* yellow roses blooming –
> > a frog
> > > at the bottom of the water.

君が地の花のつぼみを見初めけり
kimi ga ji no hana no tsubomi o misome keri

> It's the first time
> > I have seen the flowers bud
> > > in the new emperor's reign[30].

春雨の降るにも思ひおもはれう
harusame no furu ni mo omoi omowareu

> Spring rain
> > falling –
> > > many thoughts come to mind.

---

[30]　君が地 refers to the emperor's reign and clearly there is a new emperor.

秋立や富士を後ろに旅帰り
akidachi ya fuji o ushiro ni tabi kaeri

> The beginning of spring –
>> returning from a trip
>>> to the far side of Fuji.

残る火燵まだ山里はこころかな
nokoru kotatsu mada yamazato wa kokoro kana

> *Kotatsu*[31] remain yet
>> in the mountain village –
>>> the heart of things.

行く春を夜を寝ぬ顔の籬かな
yukuharu o yo o nenu kao no magaki kana

> Face unshaven[32],
>> unable to sleep –
>>> an evening in fading spring.

---

[31] A table with a futon over the frame and charcoal brazier underneath, to sit around and keep warm.
[32] Literally "roughly woven fence," I have assumed the metaphor.

42

うち晴て障子も白し春日影
uchi harete shouji mo shiroshi haru hikage

At home in fine weather –
the *shoji*[33] are white
in the spring sunshine.

山吹にさきだつ雨やみのひとつ
yamabuki ni sakidatsu ame ya mino hitotsu

I'm off in the rain
in my straw raincoat
to view *yamabuki* yellow roses.

止められぬ又来さしませ花ちらば
tomerarenu mata ki sa shimase hana chiraba

They haven't stopped!
Blossoms continue
to scatter and fall.

_____

[33]   A sliding door or partition in a Japanese house, usually with white
translucent panels.

樹の奥に滝も音して花や咲く
ki no oku ni taki mo oto shite hana ya saku

> In the depths of the woods,
>> the sound of the waterfall mingles
>>> with flowers in bloom.

肩に風裾に散して山桜
kata ni kaze suso ni chishite yamazakura

> I lean into the wind,
>> as mountain cherry blossoms scatter
>>> about my feet.

春立や誰も人よりさきへ起き
harutachi ya dare mo hito yori saki e oki

> The beginning of spring!
>> Everyone gets up earlier
>>> than he does.

春の日や庭に雀の砂あびて
haru no hi ya niwa ni suzume no suna abite

> A spring day!
>> Sparrows in the garden
>>> sand bathing.

花桶や千代の名だての初冠
hanaoke ya chiyo no nadate no uikaburi

> Wooden bucket of flowers –
>> coming-of-age ceremony[34]
>>> renowned for a thousand years.

らくらくと姥が屋根ふくやことし藁
rakuraku to uba ga yane fuku ya kotoshi wara

> The old woman
>> easily thatched the roof –
>>> this year's straw.

---

[34]   More commonly known as *genpuku*, presumably for Onitsura's son.

角菱の餅にありとも桃の花
tsunobishi no mochi ni ari tomo momo no hana

    The water chestnut *mochi*[35]
        also includes
           peach blossoms.

蛙鳴くこの夜忘るな旅まくら
kaeru naku kono yo wasuru na tabi makura

    Frogs are croaking –
        tonight I forgot
           my travel pillow.

人に逃げ人に馴るや雀の子
hito ni nige hito ni nareru ya suzume no ko

    Running away from people;
        getting used to people –
           the baby sparrow.

---

[35]   Rice cakes.

花と見てをられぬ水に石の雲
hana to mite o rarenu mizu ni ishi no kumo

    Flowers are not to be seen –
       in the water
          clouds of stone.

みればまた夫は囀る鳥の声
mireba mata otto wa saezuru tori no koe

    When I look again,
       I see it's a man singing –
          birdsong.

我ひとりむれつつ花の旅烏
ware hitori mure tsutsu hana no tabigarasu

    I am alone
       although in a crowd of people
          wandering among the blossoms.

夏が来た隣へたつも霞だけ
natsu ga kita tonari e tatsu mo kasumi dake

    Summer
       is coming soon,
          but there's only spring haze.

春まちに花の咲く身や東向き
haru machi ni hana no saku mi ya higashimuki

    Waiting for the flowers
       to bloom in spring,
          I face the east.

芽柳に遊ぶ鳥まだ寒げなり
meyanagi ni asobu tori mada samuke nari

    The birds still play
       in the willow catkins
          although it's grown cold.

雨雲の梅を星とも昼ながら
amagumo no ume o hoshi tomo hirunagara

    During midday
        plum blossoms are like stars
           against the rain clouds.

芽柳の奥たのもしき風情かな
meyanagi no oku tanomoshiki fuzei kana

    I'm looking forward
        to the elegant sight
           surrounded by willow catkins.

宇治に来て屏風に似たる茶つみかな
uji ni kite byoubu ni nitaru cha tsumi kana

    Come to Uji[36]
        and pick tea
           just like that on a folding screen.

---

[36]   A famous tea growing area near Kyoto.

遠う来る鐘の歩みや春がすみ
toou kuru kane no ayumi ya harugasumi

Coming from afar
the tolling of the bell
through the spring haze.

飲めやうたへ神の連理の若緑
nome ya uta e kami no renri no wakamidori

The fresh green shoots of the entwined pines
of the *kami*[37], give one to
drinking and song.

花垣や雲も和光の八重桜
hanagaki ya kumo mo wakou no yaezakura

Flowering hedges
and clouds too –
the double-flowered blossoms[38] of Wako[39].

_____

[37] Shinto deities, often associated with nature.
[38] Cherry blossoms with eight petals versus the usual five.
[39] A city in Saitama Prefecture.

去年からの此の花の頃又いつか

kozo kara no kono hana no koro mata itsuka

> It was sometime around now
>> that this flower bloomed
>>> last year.

雁鳴て夜の釣瓶に梅の花

ganmeite yoru no tsurube ni ume no hana

> In the evening,
>> wild geese cry out –
>>> plum blossoms in the well bucket.

花雪やそれを尽してそれをまつ

hana yuki ya sore o tsukushite sore o matsu

> Waiting
>> for snowy flowers[40]
>>> and for them to end.

---

[40] White blossoms that look like snow and scatter in the wind like snow.

花の香やむかしの袖に源氏雲
hana no ka ya mukashi no sode ni genjigumo

    The fragrance of flowers –
       on my old sleeves
          Genji clouds[41].

花散りて又閑なり園城寺
hana chirite mata shizuka nari onjouji

    The blossoms have fallen -
       peaceful once more
          at Onjoji Temple[42].

何くれと浮世を盗む花の陰
nanikure to ukiyo o nusumu hana no kage

    In various ways
       the shade of blossoming trees
          transcends[43] this fleeting world.

---

[41]   A pattern of clouds where the outline is a series of arcs, often found in illustration of Genji Monogatari. It was used as a design motif for various items including clothes.

[42]   The famous Miidera Temple on Lake Biwa.

[43]   The actual word here is "steal".

花ぞなら散らばや夢も抱くらん
hana zo nara chiraba ya yume mo dakuran

> When the blossoms fall
> > I will still hold on to
> > > my dreams.

茶の花や春によう似た朝日山
cha no hana ya haru ni you nita asahiyama

> Tea blossoms!
> > They resemble
> > > Mt. Asahi[44] in the springtime.

遠里の麦や菜種や朝霞
too sata no mugi ya natane ya asagasumi

> From distance villages –
> > grains and rapeseed
> > > and morning mist.

---

[44]   This reference is uncertain. Perhaps it is a local hill.

鞍上に人もおぼえず桜時
anjou ni hito mo oboezu sakura ji

    The person riding a horse
        is unaware
            it's cherry blossom season.

雲や匂ふ海も桜も富士の枝
kumo ya niou umi mo sakura mo fuji no eda

    The clouds and the shining sea,
        the cherry blossoms too
            - the boughs of Fuji.

牛健児車に落す草の露
ushigotei kuruma ni otosu kusa no tsuyu

    The cowherd boy
        leaves behind the cart –
            dew on the grass.

何迷ふ彼岸の入日人群り
nani mayou higan no irihi hitodakari

> How many have lost their way in life?
>> Hordes of people are out
>>> to watch the sun set on *higan*[45].

去年も咲きことしも咲くや桜花
kozo mo saki kotoshi mo saku ya sakurabana

> They bloomed last year
>> and they're blooming this year –
>>> cherry blossoms!

あら青の柳の糸や水の流れ
ara ao no yanagi no ito ya mizu no nagare

> Ah! The green slender branches
>> of the willow
>>> by the flowing stream.

---

[45] Buddhist observances held at spring and autumn equinoxes. The autumn observance is often referred to as *aki-higan*, the spring, just *higan*. The sun sets due west at this time.

一の洲へ都の人と馬刀とりに
ichi no hiji e miyako no hito to mate tori ni

> People from the capital
>> go to a distant sandbank
>>> and collect razor clams.

まけよ蒔け仏の種も彼岸から
make yo make hotoke no tane mo higan kara

> Sow, yes, sow,
>> seeds of the Buddha
>>> starting from *higan*[46].

何迷ふ彼岸の入り日人だかり
nani mayou higan no irihi hitodakari

> How can one lose their way
>> with the throngs out at sunset
>>> on *higan*?

---

[46] Buddhist observances held at spring and autumn equinoxes. The autumn observance is often referred to as *aki-higan*, the spring, just *higan*.

菅原やみこし太鼓の夜の音
sugawara ya mikoshi taiko no yoru no oto

> Sugawara[47]!
>> The festive night sounds
>>> of portable shrines and *taiko* drums.

永き日を遊び暮れたり大津馬
nagakihi o asobi kuretari ootsuuma

> The Otsu Station[48] pack horse
>> taking it easy
>>> after a long spring day.

桃の木へ雀吐出す鬼瓦
momo no ki e suzume hakidasu onigawara

> The roof gargoyles[49]
>> spew out sparrows
>>> to the peach tree.

---

[47] Sugawara no Michizane (845–903), a famous poet was deified after his death as Tenjin. His festival is held in early spring at plum blossom time.

[48] The last of the Tokaido stations before reaching Kyoto, in Shiga.

[49] Decorative ridge-end roof tiles bearing the face of a demon.

去年に似てどこやら霞む年の内
kozo ni nite dokoyara kasumu toshinouchi

    This year
       it's growing misty
          just like last year.

土に埋めて子の咲く花もあることか
 tsuchi ni umete ko no saku hana mo aru koto ka

    A child
       buried in the ground –
          will a flower bloom there?

鶯や梅にとまるば昔から
uguisi ya ume ni tomaruba mukashi kara

    The bush warbler!
       From ancient times
          it alights on the plum tree.

Summer

こいこいと言へど蟹が飛んゆく
koi koi to iedo hotaru ga tonde yuku

    Come here! Come here!
      I cry out –
         the fireflies fly away[50].

戀のない身にも嬉しや衣がえ
koi no nai mi ni mo ureshi ya koromogae

    I have no lover
      but I'm still glad –
         it's Change of Clothes day[51].

藪垣や卒都婆の間をとぶ蛍
yabugaki ya sotoba no ai o tobu hotaru

    Between the hedge
      and the wooden grave tablets –
         fireflies flitting.

_____

[50]   Onitsura's first haiku written at age seven.
[51]   The 1st day of the fourth lunar month for changing to summer clothes.

すず風やあちらむいたるみだれ髪
suzu kaze ya achira muitaru midare kami

    A cool breeze!
        over there, that person's
            hair is all in a tangle.

あの山もけふの暑さの行方かな
ano yama mo kyou no atsusa no yukue kana

    To that mountain too,
        today's heat
            has gone!

夕立や卒都婆のよめる鳥の糞
yuudachi ya sotoba no yomeru tori no kuso

    Pouring rain!
        as I read the grave marker
            – bird shit!

蜘の巣は暑きものなり夏木立
kumonosu wa atsu kimono nari natsu kodachi

    Spider's webs –
        hot robes
            for a summer grove.

夜を残す寝覚や夏の雪おろし
yo o nokosu nezame ya natsu no yukioroshi

    At dawn
        I awaken
            to snow blown down the mountain in summer!

淀ぶねや夏の今来る山かづら
yodobune ya natsu no ima kuru yamakazura

    Yodo River[52] boats!
        Now it's summer, here they come –
            clouds atop the mountains at dawn.

---

[52]   It runs from Lake Biwa through the Kyoto and Osaka regions.

川こえて赤き足行くかれ柳
kawa koete akaki ashi iku kare yanagi

My sunburnt legs
    cross the river and head for
        a withered willow.

春と夏と手さへ行きころもがえ
haru to natsu to te sae yuki koromogae

It's spring, it's summer,
    even your hands keep busy
        – it's Change of Clothes[53] day!

なでしこよ河原に石のやけるまで
nadeshiko yo kawahara ni ishi no yakeru made

The fringed pinks in bloom!
    until the rocks get burning hot
        in the dry riverbed.

---

[53] The 1st day of the fourth lunar month for changing to summer clothes.

なでしこよ川原に足のやけるまで
nadeshiko yo kawara ni ashi no yakeru made

The fringed pinks in bloom!
until my feet get sunburnt
in the dry riverbed.

夏の星影なつかしもくれかかる
natsu no hoshi kage natsukashi mo kure kakaru

Stars of summer –
I am drawn to them
even in the sky at twilight.

雲の峰なんぼ嵐の崩しても
kumo no mine nanbo arashi no kuzushite mo

The towering thunderclouds –
how many storms will it take
to topple them?

さはさはとはちす うごかす池の亀
sawasawa to hachisu ugokasu ike no kame

A rustling sound,
    lotus plants bobbing about
        – there's a turtle in the pond!

しら鳥の声に尾のある田植かな
shira tori no koe ni o no aru taue kana

At the end
    of rice planting –
        the cries of the white birds!

野の末やかりぎ畑をいづる月
no no sue ya karigi hatake o izuru tsuki

The new shoots coming up!
    The moon rises
        over a field of green onions.

竹の穂はむかしの馬の夢路かな
take no ho wa mukashi no uma no yumeji kana

    Bamboo shoots –
        dreaming of my horse
           of long ago.

夜を跡に灯白しほととぎす
yo o ato ni tomoshibi shiroshi hototogisu

    Traces of evening –
        the lantern shining
           and the lesser cuckoo.

鳴くせはし烏取りたる蝉の声
naku sewashi karasu toritaru semi no koe

    The incessant cries
        I thought were crows
           – the call of cicadas!

淀川に姿おもたや水車
yodogawa ni sugata omota ya suisha

    In the Yodo River[54],
      a massive form –
        the waterwheel.

涼風や虚空に満ちて松の声
suzukaze ya kokuu ni michite matsu no koe

    A cool breeze!
      Filling the void,
        the soughing of the pines.

熱田にて鱸の鱠吐きにけり
atsu ta ni te suzuki no namasu haki ni keri

    It was so hot in the fields
      that I threw up
        the pickled raw sea bass[55].

---

[54] It runs from Lake Biwa through the Kyoto and Osaka regions. Its waterwheel, used for irrigation, was well known.

[55] *Namasu:* a pickled vegetable dish often with raw fish.

凌霄や杖に老嚙む嫁が門
ryoushou ya tsue ni rou kamu yome ga mon

    The trumpet vine –
        an old woman leaning on her cane, rebuking
            her daughter-in-law at the gate.

嵐にも崩れぬ物や雲の峯
arashi ni mo kuzurenu mono ya kumonomine

    Even in a storm
        some things won't collapse –
            the towering clouds.

風になびく煙も夏の雪見かな
kaze ni nabiku kemuri mo natsu no yukimi kana

    Smoke hovering
        in the wind
            – snow viewing in summer!

露とりに起きて目をするくもりかな
tsuyutori ni okite me o suru kumori kana

    Waking up
        with watery eyes
            I think it's cloudy!

凌霄や蝉の団扇に日の相撲
ryoushou ya semi no uchiwa ni hi no sumou

    The trumpet vine!
        Fans for cicadas
            on a day of sumo wrestling.

夕立や隣在所は風吹て
yuudachi ya tonari zaisho wa kazefukite

    A sudden shower!
        All around
            the wind is raging.

波の底に我が足形の有るやらん
nami no soko ni waga ashigata no aru ya ran

> Beneath the waves
>   there ought to be
>   my footprints.

恋しらぬ女の粽不形なり
koi shiranu onna no chimaki funari nari

> The woman who's never known love –
>   her *chimaki*[56]
>   are shapeless.

この軒にあやめふくらん来月は
kono noki ni ayame fukuran raigetsu wa

> These eaves –
>   will be thatched with strands of iris[57]
>   next month.

---

[56]   A leaf-wrapped rice dumpling associated with Boys' Day.
[57]   Boy's Festival, on the 5th day of the fifth lunar month, derived from an iris festival in China and iris leaves are hung from the eaves.

夜を残す袖に枕に夏の露
yo o nokosu sode ni makura ni natsu no tsuyu

    At dawn,
        on my sleeve, on my pillow,
            the dew of summer.

破壺におもだか細く咲にけり
yaretsubo ni omodaka hosoku saki ni keri

    A threeleaf arrowhead
        is blooming slenderly
            in a broken pot.

霧の中に何やら見ゆる水車
kiri no naka ni nani yara mi yuru mizuguruma

    Through the mist
        one can just make out
            the waterwheel.

非情にも毛深き枇杷の若葉かな
hijou ni mo kebukaki biwa no wakaba kana

    The fresh young leaves
       of the fuzzy loquat –
          are they too, insentient?

しらぬ人と諷問答すゞみかな
shiranu hito to uta mondou suzumi kana

    A stranger,
       reciting *mondo*[58]
          while cooling off!

風呂ふけや蚋にさゝれし所をば
furo fuke ya buyo ni sasareshi tokoro o ba

    A late bath –
       a good spot for black flies
          to bite.

---

[58]   *Mondoka*. Waka poems in a question and answer format.

あちらむく君も物いへ郭公
achira muku kimi mo mono ie hototogisu

    Facing the other way,
        you're just another thing
            – lesser cuckoo.

青陽の空に鶴咲き花の声
sei you no sora ni tsuru saki hana no koe

    In sunny blue skies
      the cry of a crane
          is the voice of a flower.

卓麦や雲雀があがるあれさがる
kusamugi ya hibari ga agaru are sagaru

    Grasses and grains,
      rise and fall like a skylark,
         in stormy weather.

床まくら父に骨折る扇かな
toka makura chichi ni honeoru ougi kana

> Lying in bed,
> > the father energetically
> > > fans himself.

香盤の煙も暑き庵かな
kouban no kemuri mo atsuki iori kana

> At my retreat
> > the smoke from the incense burner
> > > is hot too.

虎御前今はつめたし石の肌
tora goze ima wa tsumetashi ishi no hada

> Tora Gozen[59]
> > now,
> > > has stone-cold skin.

---

[59]   (c1172–1238). A courtesan and famous character in the *Soga Monogatari*. Often referred to as Tora Goze in haiku. A rain associated with her is a summer seasonal word.

京の町で龍がのぼるや郭公
kyou no machi de ryuu ga noboru ya kakkou

> A dragon ascends
> over the town of Kyoto –
> a cuckoo!

侘びぬれど毛虫も落ちぬ庵かな
wabi nure do kemushi mo ochinu iori kana

> It's so desolate here –
> even the caterpillars aren't falling
> about my retreat!

お多賀への道も老曽の夏木立
otaga e no michi mo oiso no natsukodachi

> The road to the Oiso summer grove[60]
> is also the way
> to Taga-taisha shrine[61].

---

[60] Attached to Okuishi shrine in Omihachiman, Shiga Prefecture.
[61] Also known as Otaga-san, in Taga, Shiga Prefecture.

魂来とて姿なけれど瓜茄子
tamashii ki tote sugatana keredo urinasubi

    Though it appears
        souls have come,
            they're just melons and eggplants.

行く水や竹に蝉鳴く相国寺
yukumizu ya take ni semi naku shoukokuji

    The stream –
        in the bamboo, cicadas calling,
            at Shokokuji Temple[62].

空に鳴くや水田の底のほととぎす
sora ni naku ya suiden no soko no hototogisu

    It's call echoing in the sky –
        the lesser cuckoo
            at the bottom of the rice paddy.

---

[62]   A famous Buddhist temple in Kyoto.

五月雨はただ降るものと覚けり
samidare wa tada furu mono to satoru keri

> I wake up!
>> It's just early summer rain
>>> falling.

五月雨に金はしめらぬ手わざかな
samidare ni kane wa shimeranu tewaza kana

> In the early summer rains
>> money doesn't get wet
>>> with skilful hands.

春はなく夏の蛙は吠えにけり
haru wa naku natsu no kaeru wa hoe ni keri

> They croak in spring –
>> but in summer
>>> the frogs bark!

五月雨にさながら渡る仁王かな
samidare ni sanagara wataru niou kana

Being out in the early summer rains,
  is just like passing between
    the two wrathful deities[63].

五月雨を跡に置つつ有馬菅
samidare o ato ni okutsutsu ari masuga

Following
  the early summer rains –
    sedges[64].

春の夜の面ざしもなし夏の月
haru no yo no menzashi mo nashi natsu no tsuki

Those expressions on people's faces
  on spring evenings, have vanished
    – summer moon!

---

[63] Two statues representing frightening manifestions of bodhisattvas protecting
      the entrance to many Buddhist temples. Known as Nio in Japan.
[64] *Masuga* (or *umasuge*), "horse sedge".

紙子着て見ぬ唐土の郭公
kamiko kite minu morokoshi no kakkou

Wearing my paper robe[65] –
    I can't see
        the Chinese cuckoo[66].

あぢきなや広げぬ文にとぶ蛍
ajikina ya hirogenu bun ni tobu hotaru

Oh no!
    The firefly is flying
        into a rolled up scroll.

後に飽く蚊にもなぐさむ端居かな
ato ni aku ka ni mo nagusamu hashii kana

Relaxing on the veranda,
    but afterwards,
        I get fed up with the mosquitoes.

---

[65] A thin outer garment worn in winter to protect against the wind.
[66] Perhaps the Oriental cuckoo as opposed to the common cuckoo (*kakkou*) or lesser cuckoo (*hototogisu*).

雲水や庭行水に落ちかかる
unsui ya niwa gyouzui ni ochikakaru

    The itinerant monk –
       water splashing about
          as he bathes in the garden.

夏草に身をほめかれて旅の末
natsukusa ni mi o homekarete tabi no sue

    My journey ended,
       I admire
          the summer grass[67].

鵜とともに心は水をくぐり行く
u totomoni kokoro wa mizu o kuguri iku

    Together with the cormorant,
       my heart dived
          into the water.

---

[67]   "Grass" as in "grass pillow" (*kusamakura*) is associated with travel which may have been a trigger for this haiku.

夏菊に馴染初めたる大野かな
natsu giku ni najimi sometaru oono kana

    I am beginning to get familiar
        with the summer chrysanthemums
            of Ono[68].

我むかし踏みつぶしたる蝸牛かな
ware mukashi fumi tsubushitaru kagyuu kana

    A long time ago,
        I stepped on and crushed
            a snail.

何の木と見えて雨降る今宵かな
nanno ki to miete ame furu koyoi kana

    What trees
        can be seen
            on this rainy evening?

---

[68]   In modern day Fukui Prefecture.

郭公耳摺払ふ峠かな
kakkou mimi suri harau touge kana

A cuckoo's song strikes my ear
    as I dust myself off
        along the mountain pass.

蚊をよけて親の鼾や郭公
ka o yokete oya no ibiki ya kakkou

I leave behind the mosquitoes
    and the snoring of my parents –
        the cuckoo!

我に喰せ椎の木もあり夏木立
ware ni kuse shiinogi mo ari natsu kodachi

The summer grove
    has chinquapin[69] trees –
        food to eat!

---

[69] *Castanopsis cuspidata*, which has edible nuts (when cooked). As well, shiitake mushrooms, which take their name from the tree (*shii*), grow on the fallen trunks.

五月雨や鮓の重しもなめくじり
samidare ya sushi no omoshi mo name kujiri

    Early summer rains –
        on the sushi pressing stone[70]
           a slug!

うかるるや扇隣に水の花
ukaruru ya ougi tonari ni mizu no hana

    An enjoyable moment –
        fanning myself
           beside the lotus blossoms.

花と実の中垣涼し梨子の窓
hana to mi no nakagaki suzushi nashigo no mado

    Flowers and fruits
        by the fence on a cool day;
           a pear tree by the window.

---

[70]   When making sushi a stone weight was used for pressing it.

我はまだ浮世を脱がで更衣
ware wa mada ukiyo o nu ga de koromogae

    I have yet
        to take off this fleeting world –
           Change of Clothes day[71].

夏の日のうかんで水の底にさへ
natsu no hi no ukande mizu no soko ni sae

    Even the summer sun
        is floating
           at the bottom of the cool water.

ゆひ髪や鏡はなれて朝涼
yui kami ya kagami wa narete asasuzu

    Doing up my hair
        in the mirror,
           I get used to the morning chill.

---

[71]   The 1st day of the fourth lunar month for changing to summer clothes.

いさましや人の顔照る神祭
isamashi ya hito no kao teru kamimatsuri

    Inspiring!
        the shining faces of the people
           at the *kami* festival[72].

何もかも知らぬ顔せよ呼子鳥
nanimo ka mo shiranu kao seyo yobukodori

    I have no idea
        what it looks like
            – that bird I hear.

あたご火やむれつつ暮を花盛
atagohi ya muretsutsu kure o hanazagari

    The Atago Fire Festival[73],
        a myriad lanterns at sunset –
           flowers in full bloom.

---

[72]   A Shinto festival where people worship the *kami* (a god or gods).
[73]   Held on July 31 on Mt. Atago (Atago Shrine), just outside Kyoto. The deity both provides fire and helps protect against fires. A line of lanterns leads to the top.

一日で花に久しき袷かな

tsuitachi de hana ni hisashiki awase kana

The first day of the fourth month[74] –
    it's been a long time
        since I've worn my flowered kimono.

夏菊に露を打ちたる家ゐかな

natsugiku ni tsuyu o uchitaru iei kana

Spending my time at home
    I keep knocking the dew
        off the summer chrysanthemums.

夏の日を事とも瀬田の水の色

natsu no hi o koto tomo seta no mizu no iro

The colour of the Seta's[75] water
    together with
        the summer sun.

---

[74]   The fourth lunar month, in fact Change of Clothes day.
[75]   The Yodo River name in Shiga Prefecture.

わらべ達皮は味ないぞ真桑瓜

warabetachi kawa wa aji nai zo makuwauri

> The children
>> find the oriental melon's skin
>>> tasteless[76].

雨ぞ降る寝て橘の起きてもぞ

ame zo furu nete tachibana no okite mo zo

> Even if it's raining and I'm sleeping
>> I'll get up
>>> for the mandarin orange[77] blossoms.

雨雲の影神々し傘の下

amagumo no kage kougoushi kasa no shita

> Under the umbrella –
>> the divine portent
>>> of the rain clouds.

---

[76] The melon can be eaten whole, skin and all.

[77] *Tachibana*, a mandarin orange tree indigenous to Japan with inedible raw fruit but noted for the fragrance of its blossoms.

夏草のひとり花ゆれ水鏡
natsukusa no hitori hana yure mizukagami

   Reflected in the water,
     a lone flower sways
       on the summer grass.

なんとけふの暑さはと石の塵を吹く
nanto kyou no atsusa wa to ishi no chiri o fuku

   What!
     Today's heat is blowing
       dust from the rocks.

またもこん梢の海を夏の花
matamo kon kozue no umi o natsu no hana

   Once again
     tips of branches reflected in the blue sea –
       blossoms of summer.

ふところに花こそ匂へ夏の雲
futokoro ni hana koso nioi e natsu no kumo

The summer clouds
   give rise to the fragrance of flowers
      in my bosom.

ほととぎす馬追船頭お乳の人
hototogisu umaoi sendou ochi no hito

The lesser cuckoo!
   Just like the boatman, horse
      and nanny[78].

なまじひに幾夜むかしの郭公
namajii ni ikuyo mukashi no kakkou

A few evenings ago,
   the cuckoo
      sang halfheartedly.

---

[78] In Edo Japan these three were seen as representatives of someone whose
behaviour is tyrannical, either selfish or verbal and rough. The horse would
be one carrying goods or people. Onitsura seems to have had mixed feelings
about the lesser cuckoo (*hototogisu*).

飛ぶ鮎の底に雲ゆく流かな
tobu ayu no soko ni kumo yuku nagare kana

> That drifting cloud
>   looks like the bottom
>   of a flying sweetfish.

罪ふかき女めでたし土用干
tsumifukaki onna medetashi doyouboshi

> The sinful woman
>   airs
>   her wonderful summer clothes.

のり懸や橘匂ふ塀の内
norikake ya tachibana niou hei no uchi

> Riding a pack horse –
>   from within the fence
>   the fragrance of mandarin orange blossoms[79].

---

[79] Written on a journey to his hometown.

橘はその日その日のむかしかな
tachibana wa sono hi sono hi no mukashi kana

    Mandarin orange blossoms –
        that day, that day
            of long ago.

壁一重雨をへだてつ花あやめ
kabe hitoe ame o hedatetsu hana ayame

    Separated
        from the iris blossoms
            by a wall of rain.

秋は先づこの宿夕べ朝ぼらけ
aki wa mazu kono yado yuube asaborake

    At this overnight lodging,
        at daybreak,
            it will be autumn.

うぐひすは山ほととぎすばかりなり
uguisu wa yama hototogisu bakari nari

The bush warbler!
    It turns out to be
        just a mountain cuckoo.

Autumn

秋風の吹きわたりけり人の顔
aki kaze no fuki watari keri hito no kao

    The autumn wind
        blowing crosswise –
            the looks on people's faces[80]!

行水の捨所なき虫の声
gyouzui no sutedokoro naki mushi no koe

    Where I usually throw
        the bath water –
            the chirping of insects!

ながき夜を疝気ひねりて旅寝かな
nagakii yo o senki hinerite tabine kana

    A long night –
        tossing and turning with abdominal pain
            at the inn!

---

[80] While walking along a path through the fields.

つく杖のしち九にあゆめ百千鳥
tsuku tsue no shichi ku ni ayume momochidori

    With their canes,
        a few out walking
           amidst the myriad birds.

竈馬鳴く猫は竈に眠るかな
kamadoba naku neku wa kamado nemuru kana

    The hearth-cricket chirps on
        while the cat, behind the hearth,
           is sound asleep!

面白さ急には見えぬすゝきかな
omoshiro sa kyuu ni wa mienu suzuki kana

    That's something!
        suddenly I don't see it –
           the sea bass.

懶 はおぼろ烏の寝ざめかな
monogusa wa oboro karusa no ne zame kana

I feel tired,
    but the crows in the mist
        have awakened me!

どう寝ても慥な秋の寝覚かな
dou nete mo tashina aki no ne satoru kana

While I was still sleeping,
    there is no doubt, slumbering autumn
        woke up!

あゝ蕎麦ひとり茅屋の雨を臼にして
aa soba hitori kayaya no ame o usu ni shite

Ah! alone in my cottage on a rainy day
    pounding the buckwheat
        in the mortar[81].

_____

[81] Making the first soba (buckwheat noodles) in late autumn.

ともし火やおのれ顔なる雨の月
tomoshibi ya onore kao naru ame no tsuki

> The lantern!
> > One's face becomes
> > > a faint moon seen through the rain.

にょっぽり[82]と秋の空なる富士の山
nyopporito aki no sora naru fuji no yama

> Rising up
> > into the autumn sky
> > > – Mt. Fuji!

古城や茨くろなるきりぎりす
kojou ya ibara kuro naru kirigirisu

> The ancient castle[83]!
> > From the black thornbush
> > > the chirping of katydids.

---

[82] An alternative to the more common "にょっきり". Recited at the grave of a friend whose last wish was to see Mt. Fuji.

[83] Arioka Castle, an abandoned castle in Onitsura's hometown, Itami.

その秋の覚えはなかば富士の空
sono aki no oboe wa nakaba fuji no sora

    The memory of that autumn –
      Fuji thrusting
        right up to the sky.

しら糸や稲負勢鳥呼子鳥
shira ito ya inaoose sei dori yobukodori

    White threads[84]!
      – flocks of rice birds[85]
        and song birds[86].

蟷螂の鎌をたつるも力味ぞや
kamakiri no kama o tatsuru mo riki mi zoya

    Even the mantis,
      wielding its sickle,
        has the tang of power!

---

[84]   Perhaps an allusion to thin twisted *mochi* dough, known as "white threads", that the mature rice plant resembles.

[85]   One of the three traditional birds (三鳥). Variously identified, it arrives at rice harvest time. A likely candidate is the wagtail.

[86]   Another of the three traditional birds, likely a cuckoo, which is usually associated with spring.

木にも似ずさても小さき榎の実かな
ki ni mo nizu sate mo chiisaki enoki no mi kana

　　It doesn't look like that tree,
　　　　but there's the small
　　　　　　hackberry fruit!

梅をしる心もおのれ鼻もおのれ
ume o shiru kokoro mo onore hana mo onore

　　With one's heart,
　　　　with one's nose,
　　　　　　one knows the plum blossoms.

二里いぬる門に立ちたつ芽子の月
ni ri inuru mon ni tachi tatsu hagi no tsuki

　　Two miles past my gate –
　　　　bush clover standing
　　　　　　in the moonlight.

富士川や目高ほしさに秋の空
fujikawa ya medaka hoshisa ni aki no sora

The Fuji River!
    The stars are eyes, high
        in the autumn sky!

油さしあぶらさしつゝ寝ぬ夜かな
aburasashi aburasashi tsutsu nenu yo kana

Adding oil to the lamp;
    again adding oil to the lamp
        – unable to sleep tonight!

破芭蕉やぶれぬ時もばせをかな
yabu bashou yaburenu toki mo base o kana

Torn leaves of the banana plant –
    even if they're not torn,
        it's still a banana plant[87].

---

[87] The Japanese banana plant which doesn't bear fruit and whose leaves are
      easily torn in the autumn winds. Basho assumed his literary name after this
      plant.

露の玉いくつ持たる薄ぞや
tsuyu no tama ikutsu jitaru susuki zoya

    Drops of dew –
        how many can it hold?
           The pampas grass!

伏見人唐黍がらを束ねけり
fushimi hito toukibigara o tabane keri

    People from Fushimi[88]
        bind their sorghum
           in a bundle.

伏見には町屋の裏に鳴く鶉
fushimi ni wa machiya no ura ni naku uzura

    In Fushimi,
        behind a merchant's house,
           a quail is crowing.

---

[88]   Now a ward of Kyoto.

筆にとらぬ人もあらうか今日の月
ude ni toranu hito mo arau ka kyou no tsuki

    Is there anyone, I wonder,
       not taking up their writing brush?
          – tonight's moon.

野ばなれや風に吹き来る虫の声
nobanare ya kaze ni fuki kuru mushi no koe

    The distant field!
       The cries of insects
          carried along by the wind.

落穂拾ひ鶉の糞は捨てにけり
ochibo hiri uzura no fun wa sute ni keri

    Gather up the gleanings –
       but be sure to throw away
          the quail droppings!

さもかうも香さへ菊さへいつもさへ
samo kau mo ka sae kiku sae itsumo sae

    United as one,
        the fragrance and the chrysanthemums –
        always.

この露をまちて寝たぞや起きたぞや
kono tsuyu o machite neta zoya okita zoya

    Waiting for the dew –
        I fell asleep!
           I woke up!

名月や雨戸を明けて飛出づる
meigetsu ya amado o akete tobidazuru

    The harvest moon!
        the shutters slide open
           and it suddenly appears!

馬はゆけど今朝の富士見る秋路かな
uma wa yuke do kesa no fuji miru akimichi kana

    The horse treads onward –
        I'm on an autumn journey
            to see Fuji this morning.

名月やひがし半分かたぶかず
meigetsu ya higashi hanbun katabukazu

    Harvest moon!
        It's eastern half
            is no longer dark.

板渡る人にみするや草の露
ita wataru hito ni misuru ya kusa no tsuyu

    The dew on the grass
        fascinates the woman
            crossing the plank.

名月や僅かの闇を山の端に

meigetsu ya wazuka no yami o yama no ha ni

> Harvest moon!
>> A little darkness
>>> along the edge of the mountain.

箔のない釈迦に深しや秋の色

haku no nai shaka ni fukashi ya aki no iro

> The ungilded Buddha
>> in the depths of autumn
>>> amongst the fall colours[89].

目をさませ後しらぬ世の紅葉狩

me o samase nochi shiranu yo no momijigari

> The eye that wakens late
>> doesn't know the world
>>> of autumn-leaf viewing.

---

[89] Written at the former hermitage of Gensei (1623–1668), a Nichiren Buddhist monk well-known for his literary accomplishments.

琵琶の音は月の鼠のかぶりけり
biwa no oto wa tsuki no nezumi no kaburi keri

    The sound of the *biwa*[90] –
        the gnawing
            of the moon mouse[91].

旅の日はどこらにやある秋の空
tabi no hi wa dokora ni ya aru aki no sora

    The day I set out on my journey –
        where is
            the sky of autumn?

幽霊の出所はあり薄原
yuurei no dedokoro wa ari susukibara

    Where do ghosts
        come from?
            – pampas grass fields.

---

[90] Japanese lute often associate with blind Buddhist monks playing Tales of Heike or sermons.

[91] From a Buddhist text, the Parable Sutra which has two mice (or rats), white and black, representing the sun and moon, or transitoriness, who gnaw on tree roots where a traveller seeks shelter in a well. The mice often appear in literature. There could be a connection between the moon mouse and what an itinerant Buddhist monk is reciting to *biwa* accompaniment.

野の花や月夜うらめし闇ならよかろ

nonohana ya tsukiyo urameshi yami nara yokaro

    Wildflowers!
        On moonlit nights, the despised darkness
            turns out fine.

仏にも足には馴る糸瓜かな

hotoke ni mo ashi ni wa nareru hechima kana

    It's even familiar
        with the Buddha's feet
            – the sponge gourd.

白く候紅葉の外は奈良の町

shiroku soro momiji no soto wa nara no machi

    It's the white season[92]
        but it's autumn colours
            outside the town of Nara.

---

[92]   White is the colour associated with autumn in traditional Chinese and Japanese culture.

八雲立つ京に秋立つ富士にたつ
yakumo tatsu kyou ni aki tatsu fuji ni tatsu

    Rising over Fuji,
        rising in autumn over Kyoto
           – thick clouds.

女郎花猿にも馴る山路かな
ominaeshi saru ni mo nareru yamaji kana

    The golden lace
        as well as the macaque, is familiar
           with the mountain path.

石山のいしの形もや秋の月
ishiyama no ishi no nari mo ya aki no tsuki

    The shapes of the rocks
        on Stony Mountain –
           autumn moon.

虫も鳴き月も更けたり忌の内
mushi mo naki tsuki mo fuketari imi no uchi

    During the mourning period,
      both the moon and chirping insects,
        are late.

虫籠を買うて裾野にむかひけり
mushikago o kaute susono ni mukai keri

    An insect cage –
      I bought one at a shop
        facing the foot of the mountain.

吹くからに薄の露の⊏ばるるよ
fuku kara ni susuki no tsuyu no koboruru yo

    Because it's blowing,
      dew is dripping off
        the pampas grass.

朝も秋夕べも秋の暑さかな
asa mo aki yuube mo aki no atsusa kana

 The heat!
  Both on autumn mornings
   and autumn evenings.

人の親の来るとばかりや魂まつり
hito no oya no kuru to bakari ya tama matsuri

 That person's parents
  will be coming
   – Festival of the Dead[93].

只の夜の夢の枕や月の昼
tada no yo no yume no makura ya tsuki no hiru

 It was only a dream at night
  as I slept –
   a moon at noon.

___

[93] Tama Matsuri, another appellation for Bon Matsuri (Festival), where one welcomes back the spirits of one's ancestors.

後の月入りて顔よし星の空
nochi no tsuki irite kao yoshi hoshi no sora

> The ninth month moon[94] arrives –
>> the splendid face
>>> of the starry sky.

おもひやる只の秋さへくらされぬ
omoiyaru tada no aki sae kurasarenu

> I can't spend my whole day
>> just thinking
>>> about autumn.

秋風を我もの顔や旅袋
akikaze o ware mo no kao ya tabibukuro

> The autumn breeze,
>> blowing on my face
>>> and travel bag too.

---

94   The second harvest moon on the 13th day of the ninth lunar month.

111

古郷をまねくか尾花二子山

furusato o maneku ka obana futagoyama

> Does the pampas grass
>> of Mt. Futagoyama[95]
>>> entice you back to your hometown?

行く水に浮世の月もきのふかな

yukumizu ni ukiyo no tsuki mo kinou kana

> Last night,
>> the moon of this fleeting world,
>>> in the flowing stream.

秋もはや宇陀の炭竈煙りけり

aki mo wa ya uda no sumigama kemuri keri

> It's autumn again!
>> Smoke is rising
>>> from the charcoal stoves of Uda[96].

---

[95] Near Hakone, Kanagawa Prefecture.
[96] Now a city in Nara Prefecture.

魂に玉消ぬ仏に萩の露
tamashii ni tama shounu futsu ni hagi no tsuyu

    The Buddha's ever-present
       jewel in the soul –
          dew on the bush clover.

うづら鳴く吉田とほれば二階から
uzura naku yoshida to horeba nikai kara

    In Yoshida[97],
       a Japanese quail crows
         as it poops from the second floor.

かうようや月の其の空水の月
kauyou ya tsuki no sono sora mizu no tsuki

    It's inspiring!
       The moon in the water
         is that moon in the sky.

---

[97]   Now a city in Shizuoka Prefecture.

駒引の跡猶はやし梅の陰
komahiki no ato nao hayashi ume no kage

    Tracks of the horses[98]
        remain in the woods
           under the shade of the plum trees.

秋のこころ咲かぬ華見つ山桜
aki no kokoro sakanu hana mitsu yamazakura

    The spirit of autumn –
        gazing on the mountain cherry trees
           when they are not in bloom.

月影や雲居はきえず鳥の跡
tsuki kage ya kumoi wa kiezu tori no ato

    Moonlight!
        The clouds have vanished –
           bird tracks.

---

[98]   From the ceremonial presentation of horses to the emperor from outlying
farms known as *Komahiki*.

駒引の心に叶ふ旅出かな
komahiki no kokoro ni kanau tabide kana

The spirit of the horse tribute[99].
My dream come true
– now I depart.

行く秋やむかしをからで富士ひとり
yuku aki ya mukashi o kara de fuji hitori

The end of autumn!
Since ancient times
there's only been one Fuji.

月をとて漸く雲のちぎれちぎれ
tsuki o tote youyaku kumo no chigirechigire

The moon!
finally the clouds
are scattered to tiny fragments.

---

[99] The ceremonial presentation of horses to the emperor from outlying farms known as *Komahiki*.

秋や今朝たつを真袖に三津柏
aki ya kesa tatsu o ma sode ni mitsukashiwa

> Autumn begins this morning –
>> on my sleeves
>>> the three leaf[100] crest.

此の秋は膝に子のない月見かな
kono aki wa hiza ni ko no nai tsukimi kana

> This autumn
>> viewing the moon
>>> with no child on my knee.

愚痴ぐちとひとりにふける月見かは
guchi guchi to hitori ni fukeru tsukimi ka wa

> Grumbling along:
>> "Do I have to go moon gazing
>>> all by myself?"

---

[100] The *mitsukashiwa, a* common three-leaf (beech) design used as a family crest.

宗因は春死なれしが秋の塚
souin wa haru shinareshi ga aki no tsuka

    Soin[101]
        died in the spring –
            autumn's tomb.

鹿の音や渦にまひこむ浪颪
shika no ne ya uzu ni mahikomu nami oroshi

    The cry of a deer
        totally petrified in the swirls
            of the swelling waves.

秋の月人の国まで光りけり
aki no tsuki hito no kuni made hikari keri

    The autumn moon
        shines too
            upon foreign lands.

---

[101]   Soin (1605–1682), founder of the Danrin school and teacher of Onitsura.

魂棚や蚊は血ぶくれて飛びありく
tamadana ya ka wa chi bukurete tobi ariku

    The *tamadama*[102] –
        mosquitoes fly about
            giving bloody bites.

うつゝなの夜とは秋とは今ぞ嘸
utsutsuna no yo to wa aki to wa ima zo sazo

    What's certain this evening
        is that it is now
            autumn.

秋はものの月夜烏はいつも鳴く
aki wa mono no tsuki yo garasu wa itsumo naku

    When it's autumn,
        crows always caw
            on a moonlit night.

---

[102] A shelf put up for offerings to one's ancestors during the Bon Festival.

行く馬の跡に花なし菊の空
iku uma no ato ni hananashi kiku no sora

    In the tracks of the horses
        there are no flowers –
            chrysanthemum[103] in the sky!

久かたや朝のよるから空の菊
hisakata ya asa no yoru kara sora no kiku

    The heavens –
        from morning to evening
            chrysanthemum in the sky.

古寺や栗をいけたる橡の下
furudera ya kuri o iketaru tochi no shita

    An ancient temple.
        In the soil under the horse chestnut
            – chestnuts!

---

[103] Chrysanthemums were a symbol the sun.

秋の日や不二の嶺変の朝朗
aki no hi ya fuji no mine hen no asaboraka

    An autumn day!
        Over Fuji's remarkable peak
           – sunrise.

春は吉野秋は花ぞも奥の月
haru wa yoshino aki wa hana zo mo oku no tsuki

    In spring it's Yoshino[104].
        In autumn, the flowers are
           the moon.

桐の葉は落ても下に広がれり
kiri no ha wa ochite mo shita ni hirogareri

    The paulownia leaves[105] fall
        and cover the ground
           under the tree.

---

[104] The ancient area around Nara, famous in literature for its blossoms.
[105] Paulownia leaves are quite large.

御所柿のさも赤々と木の空に
goshogaki no samo akaaka to ki no sora ni

> The *Gosho* persimmons
> > on the tree
> > > are bright red against the sky[106].

風もなき秋の彼岸の綿帽子
kaze mo naki aki no higan no wataboushi

> A windless day –
> > the women's white headgear[107]
> > > of autumn *higan*[108].

犬つれて稲見に山れば露の玉
inu tsurete inemi ni dereba tsuyu no tama

> When you go out,
> > leading your dog, to view the rice plants,
> > > there will be dewdrops.

---

[106] Written after viewing a painting of gibbons.
[107] Usually made of white cotton. One kind was worn by elderly women. Another became the standard headdress for brides.
[108] A Buddhist holiday at spring and autumn equinox where one reflects on one's life and venerates one's ancestors.

秋の夢老女も遊屋も我もまた
aki no yume roujo mo yuya mo ware mo mata

   Dreams of autumn –
      one more time
         me, the brothel, the old woman.

幾露と朝待つ菊の笑顔かな
iku tsuyu to asa matsu kiku no egao kana

   So much dew!
      Waiting in the morning
         for the smiling faces of chrysanthemums.

ゆがんだよ雨の後ろの女郎花
yuganda yo ame no ushiro no ominaeshi

   They're all bent over!
      The golden lace out back
         in the rain.

出でていなば影法師もな須磨の月
dedete inaba kageboushi mo na suma no tsuki

> Leaving for Inaba,
> > my shadow too,
> > > – moon of Suma[109].

又五つ老ても光れ星の秋
mata itsutsu rou temo hikare hoshi no aki

> Even for only five old people,
> > they again shine –
> > > the autumn stars.

わが裾は三河の露と交りけり
waga suso wa mikawa no tsuyu to majiri keri

> The hem of my garment
> > is wet with the dew
> > > of Mikawa[110].

---

[109] The famous beach near Osaka. Inaba is possibly Inaba Province, now part of Tottori Prefecture.

[110] An old province of Japan, now Aichi Prefecture.

雁がねの跡に飛び行くむら烏
gan ga ne no ato ni tobi iku mura karasu

> After the geese go to sleep,
>   the crows
>   fly to the village.

吉野気の離れて白し秋の雲
yoshino ki no hanarete shiroshi aki no kumo

> White clouds of autumn
>   in the distance
>   of the Yoshino[111] sky.

ありの実のありとは梨子の花香かな
arinomi no ari to wa nashigo no kakou kana

> The fragrance of the blossoms
>   of the pear tree
>   is its true fruit[112].

---

[111] The ancient area around Nara, famous in literature for its blossoms.
[112] The phrase "*arinomi*" (fruit of existence) for pear fruit was coined to avoid the negative connotations of "*nashi*" (without), a homonym for "pear".

雨だれや暁がたに帰る雁
amadare ya akatsukigata ni kaeru kari

> Raindrops dripping from the eaves –
> > around dawn
> > > wild geese returning.

むかしやら今やらうつつ秋の暮
mukashi yara ima yara utsutsu aki no kure

> In days of old,
> > and right now –
> > > the autumn sunset!

闇の夜も又おもしろや水の星
yami no yo mo mata omoshiro ya mizu no hoshi

> In the darkness of night
> > once more it's captivating –
> > > the flickering stars[113].

_____

[113]   My interpretation of "stars of water" (水の星).

我れが身に秋風寒し親ふたり
ware ga mi ni akikaze samushi oya futari

> My parents and I
>> are cold
>>> out in the autumn wind.

うき島や露に香うつる馬の腹
ukishima ya tsuyu ni ka utsuru uma no hara

> Ukishima[114] –
>> The fragrant dew
>>> reflects the horse's belly.

影法師に心を分ける月見かな
kageboushi ni kokoro o wakeru tsukimi kana

> Moon viewing!
>> My heart's split in two –
>>> one part in my shadow[115].

---

[114] Unknown. Literally "floating island". There is an island of this name in Tokyo Bay.
[115] Written on the 15th night (the night of the full moon).

稲妻や淀の与三右が水車
inazuma ya yodo no yasau ga mizuguruma

    Lightning!
        On the Yodo River[116], three quick flashes to the right,
            lighting up the waterwheel.

ななくさや露の盛りを星の花
nanakusa ya tsuyu no sakari o hoshi no hana

    The seven autumn flowers[117]
        and dew at its peak –
            star flowers!

ひらひらと木の葉うごきて秋ぞ立
hirahira to konoha ugokite aki zo ritsu

    The leaves on the trees
        are fluttering and swaying –
            autumn has begun.

---

[116] It runs from Lake Biwa through the Kyoto and Osaka regions. Its waterwheel, used for irrigation, was well known.

[117] Blossoms of bush clover, pampas grass, arrowroot, fringed pink, golden lace, thoroughwort and morning glory.

まつとならいなば又こん秋もやがて
matsu to nara inaba mata kon aki mo yagate

    Waiting for it to begin –
        soon it will be autumn again
            in Inaba[118].

ふむ足や美濃に近江に草の露
fumu ashi ya mino ni oumi ni kusa no tsuyu

    My feet brush
        the dew on the grass
            in Mino and Omi provinces[119].

あらたのし冬立つ窓の釜の音
ara tanoshi fuyu tatsu mado no kama no oto

    Ah! How I enjoy
        the beginning of autumn,
            the sound of the cauldron by the window.

---

[118]   Possibly Inaba Province, now part of Tottori Prefecture.
[119]   Historical provinces. Mino is now part of Gifu Prefecture and Omi is now Shiga Prefecture.

ひよ鳥や世の囀も石の花
hiyodori ya yo no saezu mo ishi no hana

The brown-eared bulbul[120]!
Its song rings throughout –
flower of stone.

なんと菊のかなぐられうぞ枯てだに
nanto kiku no ka nagurareu zo karete dani

How can a chrysanthemum
be cut down
and left to wither?

心から栗に味ある節句かな
kokoro kara kuri ni aji aru sekku kana

Wholeheartedly,
I relish the taste of the chestnuts
at this year's festival[121].

---

[120] A long-tailed mostly grey bird.
[121] In fact, the Chrysanthemum Festival, held on the 9th day of the ninth lunar month each year.

破芭蕉破れぬ時も芭蕉かな
yabu bashou yaburenu toki mo bashou kana

    That banana plant[122] was torn,
        while at the same time,
            this one wasn't!

朝寒の今日の日南や鳥の声
asasamu no kyou no nichinan ya tori no koe

    This morning's chill
        in Nichinan[123] –
            the singing of birds.

心にて顔に向ふや魂祭
kokoro nite kao ni mukau ya tamamatsuri

    Festival of Souls[124] –
        I turn my face
            towards my heart.

---

[122] The Japanese banana plant which doesn't bear fruit and whose leaves are easily torn in the autumn winds. Basho assumed his literary name after this plant.

[123] A town in what is now Tottori Prefecture.

[124] *Tamamatsuri*, another name for the Bon or Obon Festival where one welcomes back the spirits of one's ancestors.

我祖師も舟橋おがむ秋の水
ware soshi mo funahashi ogamu aki no mizu

> My Master too, bows in reverence
> > to the floating bridge –
> > > swelling waters of autumn[125].

吹からに芒の露のこぼるるよ
fuku kara ni susuki no tsuyu no koboruru yo

> Because of the wind blowing
> > dew on the pampas grass
> > > scatters and falls.

宇治川や朝霧立ちて伏見山
ujigawa ya asagiri tachite fushimiyama

> Uji River[126]!
> > Morning mist has arisen
> > > on Mt. Fushimi[127].

---

[125] Crossing the Tenryu River in Shizuoka Prefecture while travelling to Kyoto.
[126] Flowing through Uji, south of Kyoto.
[127] More of a hill, the site of the Fushimi Inari shrine.

椴の木のすんと立ちたる月夜かな
todo no ki no sun to tachitaru tsuki yo kana

    Rising above
        the Sakhalin firs –
            the evening moon.

角ぎりや礎のこす鹿の京
tsunogiri ya ishizue nokosu shika no kyou

    Antlers cut[128]!
        Your essence left behind –
            deer of Kyoto.

---

[128] An autumn event to cut off the horns of stag deer held at Kasuga Shrine in Nara. The deer are sacred and the idea was to prevent injury to them and humans.

Winter

ひゅうひゅうと風は空ゆく冬牡丹
hyuhyu to kaze wa sora yuku fuyu botan

The wind is whistling
across the sky –
winter peonies!

しろ金や霰ふる夜の年忘れ
shirokin ya arare furu yo no toshiwasure

White gold!
Sleet falling on the evening
of the New Year's Eve party[129].

茫々と取乱したるすすきかな
boubou to torimida shitaru susuki kana

Over the wide plain,
drooping everywhere,
pampas grass!

---

[129] *Toshiwasure*, a traditional year-end drinking party.

つめたさに火を吹きおこす土火入
tsumetasa ni hi o fuki okosu tsuchi hi ire

In the cold,
blowing on the fire to get it going,
it spread to the ground.

つくづくとものゝはじまる火燵かな
tsukuduku to mono no hajimaru kotatsu kana

It's really time
to get started on things
– the *kotatsu*[130]!

ともし火の花に春まつ庵かな
tomoshibi no hana ni haru matsu iori kana

By the lanterns
patterned with flowers
– waiting for spring at my retreat!

---

[130] A table with a futon over the frame and charcoal brazier underneath, to sit around and keep warm. So winter has begun and it's time to start working on those things one does in winter.

おとなしき時雨を聞くや高野山
otonashiki shigure o kiku ya kouyasan

    In the silence,
        I listen to a quiet winter shower
            – Mt. Koya[131].

重ね着に寒さもしらぬ姿かな
kasanegi ni samusa mo shiranu sugata kana

    Wearing all these layers of clothing
        I don't even feel
            the cold.

鶯や五文字ほどく年の内
uguisu ya itsu moji hodoku toshi no uchi

    The bush warbler!
        It's unravelled five *moji*[132]
            this year!

---

[131]   Home to many Buddhist temples, notably of the Shingon sect.
[132]   Japanese letters or characters.

木がらしの音も似ぬ夜のおもひかな
kogarashi no oto mo ninu yo no omoi kana

　　The sound of the withering wind –
　　　　it doesn't feel
　　　　　　like it's nighttime.

鶯の鳴けば何やらなつかしう
uguisu no nakeba naniyara natsukashiu

　　When the bush warbler sings
　　　　I somehow
　　　　　　feel nostalgic.

ささ栗の柴に刈らるる小春かな
sasa kuri no shiba ni kararuru koharu kana

　　Cutting down the small chestnut trees
　　　　for firewood –
　　　　　　early winter[133]!

---

[133]　小春 (*koharu*), literally "little spring", means the tenth lunar month or sometimes a warm day in early winter. The latter meaning now refers to late autumn.

餅哥や君が歳暮の馬下りに
mochi uta ya kimi ga seibo no umaori ni

   Mochi and song!
      The master has arrived –
         it's New Year's Eve!

夜あらしや時雨の底の旅枕
yo arashi ya shigure no soko no tabimakura

   An evening tempest!
      Sleeping away from home,
         beneath a winter drizzle.

富士の雪我れ津の国の生れなり
fuji no yuki ware tsu no kuni no umarenari

   Snowcapped Fuji –
      I was born
         in Settsu Province[134].

---

[134] Onitsura was born in Itami, Settsu Province, now Hyogo Prefecture.

来る年の身もたのもしや枇杷の花

kuru toshi no mi mo tanomoshi ya biha no hana

> For the coming year
>> I too am hopeful –
>>> loquats[135] in bloom.

膝頭つめたい木曽の寝覚かな

hizagashira tsumetai kiso no nezame kana

> I wake up
>> in Kiso[136]
>>> with cold knees!

夜を残す風なほ寒しひとつ窓

yo o nokosu kaze naho samushi hitotsu mado

> At dawn,
>> a wind still colder
>>> by the one window.

---

[135] Loquat fruit is a symbol of good luck and wealth due to its gold colour.
[136] A town in Nagano Prefecture with cold winters and heavy snowfalls. Onitsura was staying there while on a journey.

夕陽の流石に寒し小六月
sekiyou no sasuga ni samushi korokugatsu

> As to be expected,
>> it's cold as the sun sets
>>> in "little sixth month"[137].

冬ながら人の初音や郭公
fuyunagara hito no hatsune ya kakkou

> During winter
>> he hears the first call
>>> of the cuckoo.

ちらとのみ雪は浮世の花候な
chira to no mi yuki wa ukiyo no hanakouna

> To see the snow fall –
>> it's like blossom time,
>>> in this fleeting world.

---

[137] A euphemism for the tenth lunar month.

灯火の言葉を咲かす寒さかな
tomoshibi no kotoba o sakasu samusa kana

    From the cold
       blooms the language
          of the lantern.

寝られぬやにがにが敷も鳴千鳥
nerarenu ya niganiga shiki mo naku chidori

    I can't sleep!
       It's annoying – countless birds chirping
          and its spreading.

水よりも氷の月はうるみけり
mizu yori mo kouri no tsuki wa urumi keri

    The moon of ice[138]
       is even wetter than
          water.

---

[138]   Perhaps water frozen in a pail. Issa uses this image as well.

くむ汐や千鳥残して帰る海士
kumu shio ya chidori nokoshite kaeru ama

> The fisherman
>   scoops up some water and returns home,
>   leaving the plovers behind.

水鳥のおもたく見えて浮きにけり
mizutori no omotaku miete uki ni keri

> The waterfowl
>   look heavy –
>   but they can float!

雪に笑ひ雨にも笑ふむかしかな
yuki ni warai ame ni mo warau mukashi kana

> Laughing at the snow
>   and even laughing at the rain,
>   a long time ago.

うつくしく交る中や冬椿
utsukushiku majiru naka ya fuyu tsubaki

> Beautifully
>> mingled together –
>>> winter camellia.

あたゝかに冬の日向の寒きかな
atataka ni fuyu no hinata no samuki kana

> It's warm
>> in the winter sun
>>> on this cold day.

古寺に皮むく棕櫚の寒げなり
furudera ni kawa muku shuro no samugenari

> An ancient temple,
>> a palm's trunk is peeling
>>> – the cold!

枯芦や難波入江のささら波
kare ashi ya naniwa irie no sasara nami

Withered reeds!
    The rippling waves
        of Naniwa[139] Bay.

殊勝なり牛の糞ふむ鉢叩
shushou nari ushi no kuso fumu hachitataki

Extraordinary!
    Stepping on cow dung
        sounds like striking the begging bowl[140].

吾妻路の夜露こふたる紙子かな
azuma ji no yotsuyu koutaru kamiko kana

I journeyed along the eastern road[141]
    through the night dew
        in my paper robe[142].

---

[139] The old name for Osaka.
[140] Buddhist monks struck a bowl (or gourd) when going out begging.
[141] A road leading from Kyoto to the Kanto area (Edo and Kamakura).
[142] A thin outer garment worn in winter to protect against the wind.

春待や幸ある家の花袋
haru machi ya kou aru ie no hanabukuro

    Waiting for spring[143] –
        the floral bags in the house
            will bring good luck.

お地蔵のもすそに鳴くや磯千鳥
ojizou no mosuso ni naku ya iso chidori

    From the base of Ojizo[144]
        the call of a bird –
            a beach plover!

糸に只声のこぼるる時雨かな
ito ni tada koe no koboruru shigure kana

    Just threads –
        the sound
            of the falling drizzle.

---

[143] Likely the twelfth lunar month.
[144] The Buddhist guardian of travellers and children with stone statues found throughout the country. Strictly speaking "Jizo" – the "O" is honorific.

十月の二日も我もなかりけり
juugatsu no futsuka mo ware mo nakari keri

The second day of the tenth month
and me too –
nowhere to be found[145].

春に似て心うるはし冬日和
haru ni nite kokoro uruwashi fuyubiyori

It's just like spring!
It feels so wonderful –
the winter sun.

珠数くりて春を待つこそ仕事なれ
juzu kurite haru o matsu koso shigoto nare

Counting off the rosary beads
while waiting for spring –
I'm used to it.

_____
[145]   On the 1st all the gods left for Izumo for the month.

時雨ても雫短し天王寺
shigurete mo shizuku mijikashi tennouji

    For a short while,
        early winter drizzle, water dripping
            at Tennoji Temple[146].

薫るより雪気はげしく今朝うらら
kaoru yori yuki ki hageshiku kesa urara

    It's a lovely morning,
        but the threatening snow-clouds loom larger
            than the fine fragrance.

実を底に持ちてたのもし枇杷の花
mi o soko ni mochite tanomoshi biha no hana

    Planting the seeds deep,
        hopeful of
            loquat blossoms.

---

[146] Presumably Shitennoji Temple in Osaka.

行としや市にきしろふ炭翁
yukutoshi ya ichi ni kishirou sumiokina

> End of the year!
> > In the city, the charcoal sellers
> > > fiercely competing.

花を雪に見たる法師や雪の花
hana o yuki ni mitaru houshi ya yuki no hana

> The Buddhist priest
> > saw it snow on the flowers –
> > > snow flowers!

むさし野は堂よる出る冬の月
musashino wa dou yori izuru fuyu no tsuki

> Musashino[147] –
> > the winter moon
> > > appears above a temple.

---

[147] The famous grassy plain in the Tokyo region.

河豚喰て其の後雪の降りにけり
fugu kuute sono ato yuki no furi ni keri

> I ate a blowfish[148]
>> and after that
>>> it started to snow.

叶へばぞ陽につぼめる霜の花
kanaeba zo you ni tsubomeru shimo no hana

> If my wish comes true,
>> frost flowers will bud
>>> in the sun.

井のもとの草葉に重き氷柱かな
i no moto no kusaba ni omoki tsurara kana

> Heavy icicles
>> lie amid the blades of grass
>>> about the well.

---

[148]   If not cleaned properly, eating this fish can be fatal.

鎌とぐや生駒あたりの年の暮
kama togu ya ikoma atari no toshi no kure

    The sharpened sickle!
        By the side of the Ikoma[149] River
            at the end of the year.

何ゆえに長みじかある氷柱ぞや
nani yueni naga mijika aru tsurara zoya

    Why are there
        icicles that are long
            and icicles that are short?

遠干潟沖はしら波鴨の声
tou higata oki wa shiranami kamo no koe

    Far past the tidal flats
        on the open sea, the calls of ducks
            on the breaking waves.

---

[149] In Nara Prefecture. Commonly known as the Tatsuda River.

河豚程ふくのやうなる物はなし
fukuto hodo fuku no ya unaru mono wa nashi

> A blowfish[150]
> > that has blows past its limit
> > > is nothing.

ひうひうと風は空ゆく冬ぼたん
hiuhiu to kaze wa sora yuku fuyu botan

> The wind blows fiercely
> > through the sky –
> > > winter peonies!

寒空に都を逃し物ぐるひ
amuzora ni miyako o nogashi monogurui

> To flee the capital[151]
> > in the cold weather
> > > is crazy.

---

[150] The blowfish (another name for the puffer fish) blows itself up to twice its size as a defence mechanism.
[151] Kyoto.

羽二重に降るやら松に竹に霜
habutae ni furu yara matsu ni take ni shimo

    Frost falls
       on the pines, on the bamboo –
          fine white silk.

寒苦鳥の声に脈みる山路かな
kankuchou no koe ni myaku miru yamaji kana

    The cries of the *kankucho*[152] birds
       echo along the path
          through the mountains.

むかしおもふ時雨降る夜の鍋の音
mukashi omou shigure furu yo no nabe no oto

    Thinking of long ago –
       the sound of the saucepan
          on an evening of drizzling rain.

---

[152] A pair of mythological birds in Buddhism, living in the mountains, who cry
out at the coldness of night but neglect to build a nest in the warmth of day.

皆人の匂ひはいはじ枇杷の花
minahito no nioi wa ihaji biha no hana

    I wouldn't say everyone's scent
      is that of
        loquat blossoms.

家鴨かとおもふ人なし沖の鴨
ahiru ka to omou hitonashi oki no kamo

    The domestic duck,
      thinking no one is around,
        takes to open water like a wild duck.

引かへて白い毛になる石蕗の花
hika hete shiroi ke ni naru tsuwabuki no hana

    The flowers of the leopard plant
      are drawn up
        by white hairs[153].

---

[153] The small flowers grow on long and slender light-coloured stems.

いつも見る物とは違ふ冬の月
itsumo miru mono to wa chigau fuyu no tsuki

    The one you usually see
      is different from
        the moon of winter.

はや陽の恵みて冬の笑ひかな
haya you no megumite fuyu no warai kana

    A smile in winter –
      the blessing
        of an early sun.

行としのそらの隙さへいそがしき
yuku toshi no sora no suki sae isogashiki

    It's so busy,
      even in "leisure time" –
        the end of the year.

青雲やたかの羽せせる峯の松

seiun ya taka no hane seseru mine no matsu

> Blue sky –
> > at the top of a pine,
> > > a falcon flapping its wings.

天照や梅に椿に冬日和

amaterasu ya ume ni tsubaki ni fuyubiyori

> Amaterasu[154]!
> > A mild sunny winter day
> > > with plum and camellia blossoms.

痩臑に漸く寒し大井川

yasezune ni youyaku samushi ooigawa

> Finally!
> > My skinny legs enter
> > > the cold Oigawa River[155].

---

[154] Japanese goddess of the sun, here symbolizing the sun. Written while preparing flowers for the *oharai* purification festival held on the last day of the year.

[155] This river runs from Japan's Southern Alps to Shizuoka Prefecture.

冬枯や平等院の庭の面
fuyuka ya byoudouin no niwa no men

   Winter desolation –
     the garden
       at Byodo-in Temple[156].

---

[156] A famous Buddhist temple in Uji, near Kyoto.

No Specific Season

月も雪も何か残らう花も筆に
tsuki mo yuki mo nanka nokorau hana mo fude ni

> Both moon and snow
> > and something else – flowers too!
> > > – captured by the pen[157].

気辛労や馬に乗ろ物小田原へ
kishindo ya uma ni noro mono odawara e

> It's a struggle!
> > Packing goods on the horse
> > > bound for Odawara[158].

あら涼し鉦の音死ぬ一心院
ara suzushi kane no oto shinu isshin in

> Ah! the pure sound of the bell's
> > death knell
> > > at Isshin-in[159].

---

[157] Literally "writing brush (*fude*)"
[158] Now a city in Kanagawa Prefecture.
[159] A Pure Land Buddhist temple in Kyoto.

むかし色の底に見えつつ花紅葉
mukashi iro no soko ni mietsutsu hana kouyou

Since ancient times
    flowers and autumn foliage have been seen
        as the paradigm of colour.

雲水や石な礫の端五つ
unsui ya ishina tsubute no hashi itsutsu

The itinerant monk –
    throwing five pebbles
        lying about.

はづかしや榾にふすぼる煙草頬
hazukashi ya hota ni fusuboru tabakozura

Embarrassing!
    A little kindling but black smoke pours out –
        tobacco face!

みどり立つ岸の姫松めでたさよ
midori tatsu kishi no himematsu medeta sayo

    A wonderful evening –
        the small green pines
            overlooking the coast.

春と秋とひとつに富て竹紅葉
haru to aki to hitotsu ni tomite take momiji

    Spring and autumn
        are one in their riches –
            bamboo and autumn colours.

www.ingramcontent.com/pod-product-compliance
Lightning Source LLC
Chambersburg PA
CBHW061946070426
42450CB00007BA/1074